W9-BWT-828

Snap
books®

GET IN THE GAME

A GIRL'S GUIDE TO
BASKETBALL

by Allyson Valentine Schrier

Consultant:
Pam Gohl
Head Coach, Women's Basketball
Minnesota State University, Mankato

CAPSTONE PRESS
a capstone imprint

Snap Books are published by Capstone Press,
1710 Roe Crest Drive, North Mankato, Minnesota 56003
www.capstonepub.com

 Books published by Capstone Press are manufactured with paper
containing at least 10 percent post-consumer waste.

Library of Congress Cataloging-in-Publication Data
Schrier, Allyson Valentine.
  A girl's guide to basketball / by Allyson Valentine Schrier.
    p. cm. — (Snap books. Get in the game.)
  Includes bibliographical references and index.
  Summary: "Quizzes, rules, and tips and tricks on how to play basketball"—Provided by publisher.
  ISBN 978-1-4296-7670-0 (library binding)
  1. Basketball for girls—Juvenile literature. I. Title. II. Series.

GV886.S37 2012
  796.323—dc23   2011034291

Editor: Mari Bolte
Designer: Bobbie Nuytten
Media Researcher: Eric Gohl
Production Specialist: Laura Manthe

Photo Credits:
Alamy/GPI Stock, 7 (bottom); Capstone Studio/Karon Dubke, 13, 19, 21, 25, 27, 29; Getty Images/The
Washington Post/Tracy A. Woodward, 15; Newscom/ZUMA Press/The Orange County Register/Rose
Palmisano, 5, ZUMA Press/p77, cover (right), ZUMA Press/San Diego Union-Tribune/Charlie Neuman,
17; Shutterstock/Aspen Photo, 11, 16, irabel8, 23 (left), kanate, 8, Marco Mayer, 23 (right), MarFot,
cover (top left), back cover, 2, 4–5 (top), 7 (top), 14, 18, 20 (top), 26, msheldrake, 20 (bottom), Petur
Asgeirsson, 10, Travis Manley, 22

Design Elements:
Shutterstock/Sergey Kandakov (stars), Solid (cheering crowd)

Printed in the United States of America in North Mankato, Minnesota.

122013   007916R

★ TABLE OF CONTENTS ★

★ CHAPTER 1 ★

How Much Do You Know?

Are you a queen of the court who loves nothing more than the sound of a bouncing basketball? Do you pump your fist and say, "Three points!" as you toss your laundry into the basket? Or are you new to the game and just want to learn how to walk and dribble at the same time?

In 1891 James Naismith hung a couple of peach baskets in his local YMCA. The baskets were for boys to shoot balls through. Naismith had just invented one of the most popular sports of all time. Today more than 450,000 girls in the United States play on teams throughout the country. Whatever your level of play, here's a quiz to test your hoops IQ.

1. Coach has assigned each player a girl she's supposed to guard and try to keep from scoring. This type of defense is called:

a) zone defense

b) one-on-one defense

c) no score defense

d) person-to-person defense

2. Not many school-aged girls are tall enough to do a slam-dunk. What's the height of the hoop?

a) 8 feet (2.4 meters)

b) 10 feet (3 m)

c) 12 feet (3.7 m)

d) 14 feet (4.3 m)

3. You're the tallest girl on the team and can jump the highest. No wonder the coach made you the:

a) center

b) shooting guard

c) point guard

d) jumper

4. Keep moving! You're not allowed to stay still in the lane for more than:

a) five seconds

b) 10 seconds

c) three seconds

d) one minute

5. You steal the ball and run down the court. You make a running layup shot from just beneath the basket. The crowd cheers as the ball drops through the net. How many points get added to your team's score?

a) one point

b) two points

c) three points

d) four points

6. You were taking a three-point shot when a girl from the other team fouled you. Your shot missed. How many free throw attempts do you get?

a) three

b) one

c) two

d) None. You get to take the ball in from the sideline.

7. During a game, how many girls from each team are allowed on the court?

a) seven

b) nine

c) five

d) six

8. A girl from the other team took steps without dribbling the ball. This is a traveling violation. What is the penalty?

a) Her team loses two points.

b) Your team gets to take two free throws.

c) There's no such thing as a traveling violation.

d) Your team gets to throw the ball in from out-of-bounds.

9. Basketball isn't just for giants! If you're quick on your feet and can call plays, height doesn't matter. Coach will position you as a:

a) shooting guard

b) point guard

c) forward

d) center

10. When a player double dribbles, her team loses possession of the ball. What is double-dribbling?

a) Dribbling the ball with two hands at the same time.

b) Dribbling the ball while standing still.

c) Dribbling the ball, stopping, then starting to dribble again.

d) a and c.

answers at the bottom of page 31

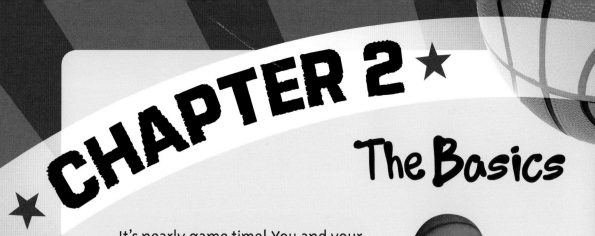

★ CHAPTER 2 ★

The Basics

It's nearly game time! You and your teammates jog onto the court. You do some stretches and run some drills. Coach calls you to the sidelines for a pregame cheer. Finally, five girls from your team head to the middle of the court. The girls who don't start the game will get the chance to play later.

The referee tosses the ball into the air. Your team's center, usually the tallest girl or best jumper, leaps for the ball. She tips the ball to a teammate. Game on! The first of four eight-minute quarters, or two 18-minute halves, are under way.

High school basketball courts are usually 84 x 50 feet (25.6 x 15.2 m).

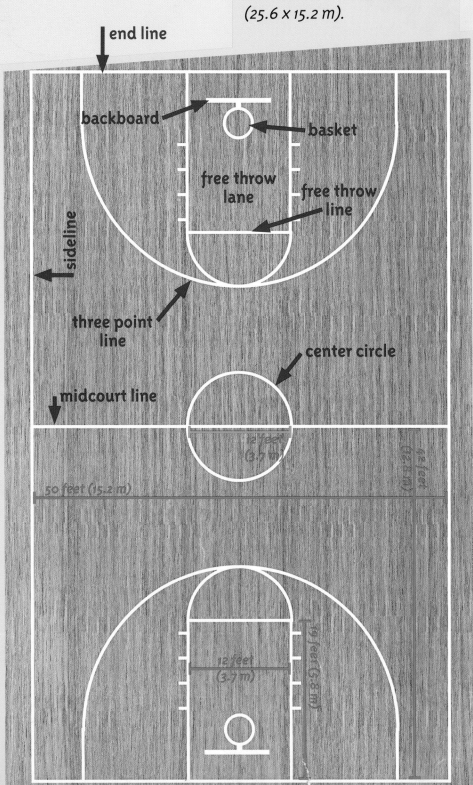

end line

backboard

basket

free throw lane

free throw line

sideline

three point line

center circle

midcourt line

12 feet (3.7 m)

12 feet (12.8 m)

50 feet (15.2 m)

12 feet (3.7 m)

19 feet (5.8 m)

Positions

Your team won the jump, so you're playing offense. You work together to get the ball down the court. Each step brings you closer to your team's basket. What you do on the court depends on your position.

GUARDS: On the short side? That's OK. Stand between the midcourt line and three-point line. You're the point guard or the shooting guard. Your quick dribbling and powerful passing skills are what matter the most. Your job is to set up plays and to take long shots. Your team is relying on you to keep opponents from getting close enough to take their own shots.

FORWARDS: Are you good at taking shots close to the basket? Can you out-jump the competition and snatch balls that rebound off the backboard? You might have what it takes to be a forward. The small forward uses speed to drive in for layups. The power forward uses her height to block the other team's shots.

CENTER: As the tallest girl on the team, you've got a big responsibility. Your job is to tip the jump ball to your teammates. Once the game is under way, you take shots close to the basket. You also nab rebounds to get the ball into your team's control.

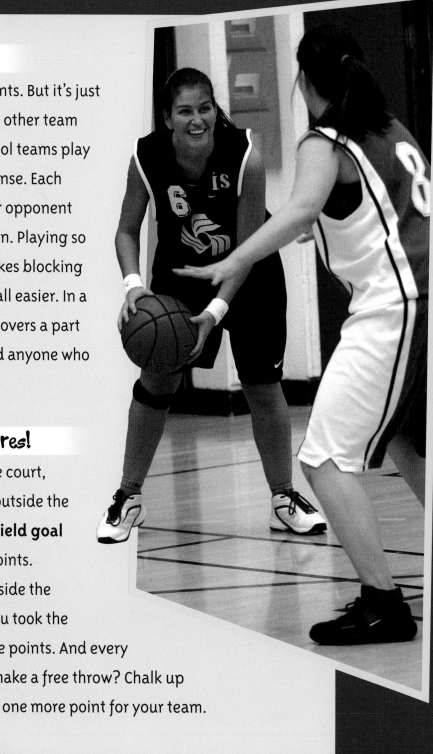

D-E-F-E-N-S-E!

It's great to score points. But it's just as important to keep the other team from scoring. Many school teams play a person-to-person defense. Each girl sticks like glue to her opponent playing the same position. Playing so closely to each other makes blocking shots and stealing the ball easier. In a zone defense, each girl covers a part of the court. They defend anyone who steps into their area.

She shoots—She scores!

You dribble down the court, release a shot from just outside the lane. Swish! It's in! That **field goal** earned your team two points. If you were standing outside the three-point line when you took the shot, you've earned three points. And every time you're fouled and make a free throw? Chalk up one more point for your team.

FIELD GOAL: a successful shot taken from the court while the game is in play

Fouls and Violations

Even the best players make mistakes. If you and your opponent get too physical, you may earn yourself a foul. Mishandle the ball or take an extra step and you've picked up a **violation**. Be sure you know which are which and the consequences of both.

Fouls

In a fast and physical game like basketball, even the nicest girls play a little rough sometimes. If you've been fouled, there are two options to choose from. Your team might take the ball in from out-of-bounds. Or you might shoot from the free-throw line. What happens depends on what you were doing when fouled. It also depends on the total number of fouls the offending team has already committed.

VIOLATION: an action that breaks the rules of a sport or game

Total number of fouls the offending team has committed:	If fouled player was NOT shooting a basket:	If fouled player was shooting a two-point basket:	If fouled player was shooting a three-point basket:
0—6	Her team inbounds the ball, throwing it in from the sideline or baseline	She takes two free throws	She takes three free throws
7—9	She takes one free throw, plus one more if she makes the first one	She takes two free throws	She takes three free throws
more than 10	She takes two free throws	She takes two free throws	She takes three free throws

Violations

Commit a violation and the other team gets to take the ball in from the sideline. Traveling, double dribbling, and smacking the ball are only a few of the violations you can receive. Here's a more in-depth look at violations:

- **Traveling**—Got the ball? You won't be able to move forward without dribbling.

- **Double dribbling**—If you stop while dribbling the ball, you can either pass or take a shot. Resume dribbling and you lose the ball. And don't dribble using two hands—that's double dribbling too.

- **Backcourt violation**—Once you've moved the ball past the midcourt line it can't be passed to a teammate still behind the midcourt line.

- **Three-second rule**—No player can stay in the lane for more than three seconds.

- Other violations include smacking the ball with a fist or kicking it, and missing the hoop, net, and backboard on a free throw

Game Over

The seconds tick down. The final buzzer rings. Game over! The team with the most points wins. But what if the scores are tied? If the score is tied, five-minute overtime periods are played. In some youth leagues, a final sudden death round is played. The first team to score wins the game.

Whether you win or lose, good sportsmanship is important when playing the game.

CHAPTER 3

Basketball Does a Body Good!

The court may not look so big from the sidelines. You may change your mind after spending 32 minutes sprinting back and forth on it! Pro players run up to 5 miles (8 kilometers) per game. All that running is a terrific workout for your heart. Jumping for shots and rebounds builds powerful leg muscles. Passing, dribbling, and blocking shots strengthen your hands and arms.

Basketball is great for strengthening bones too. You work against **gravity** as you pound down the court and make quick starts and stops. That weight-bearing exercise triggers your body to produce more bone tissue. Denser bones are a huge plus later in life.

And what about your hand-eye **coordination**? Nothing boosts it like trying to get a basketball through a hoop or around a defender!

GRAVITY: the force that pulls objects with mass together

COORDINATION: the ability to control body movements

14

Basketball Scores High Brain Points

At practice, the coach runs you through dozens of plays. During a game, you need to remember each and every one. Where should you stand? Who should you look to for a pass? Don't panic. Keep your focus!

During the game, the point guard pumps a chest pass your way. You dribble, stop, and pivot. Should you take an outside shot or pass to a teammate? Who's open for a pass? Are you too far away to make an accurate shot? It's time for some quick thinking!

After the game, you still have homework to do. Your brain is still buzzing from the game, and you breeze through your assignments. Has math always been so easy?

Memorizing plays and making quick decisions are how basketball works your mind as well as your body. These activities help you both on and off the court. Studies have shown that kids who play sports tend to do better in school than kids who don't. They also have higher self-esteem, less anxiety, are less likely to be depressed, and usually get a better night's sleep.

Basketball helps your body and mind stay sharp.

Lessons about Life

Have you ever tried palming a basketball? It would never work without all your fingers pulling together. On the court, you and your teammates are like five fingers gripping a ball. Every girl out there is an important player.

Every girl on the court needs to be giving her all. That takes commitment. Miss practice when coach is teaching a new play? You might dribble when your teammates are expecting you to pass. If you miss a game, that's one less girl available to play. That means your whole team has to work harder. Being dependable and working well with others are skills that'll stick with you on and off the court.

Play Safe, Play Smart

Back when basketball was new, girls had to worry about tripping over their dresses while making layups. Today shorts and jerseys make playing a lot easier! Still, injuries happen. Quick turns can result in sprained ankles or injured knees. Jumping for the ball might put you head-to-head with another player. Blocking a shot could send you flying across the floor.

Girls are six to 10 times more likely than boys to suffer knee injuries. Experts think that a hormone that girls produce, called estrogen, has something to do with it. **Estrogen** may loosen girls' **ligaments**, making girls more likely to get injured. In addition, the number of female players with head injuries has tripled in recent years.

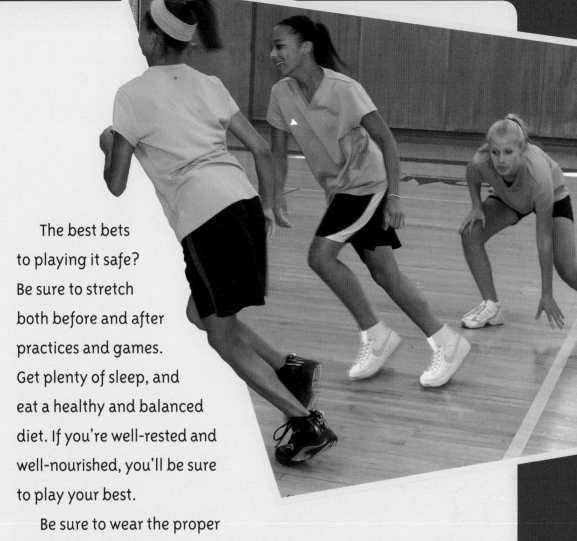

The best bets to playing it safe? Be sure to stretch both before and after practices and games. Get plenty of sleep, and eat a healthy and balanced diet. If you're well-rested and well-nourished, you'll be sure to play your best.

Be sure to wear the proper equipment during the game. A mouth guard, knee pads, and elbow pads will protect you from bumps and bruises. Sneakers with great ankle support will help you stay on your toes too.

Stay in shape both in and out of season. A fit player is less likely to get hurt. And if you're feeling tired or injured, let the coach know. It's better to sit out a single game than risk missing a whole season.

ESTROGEN: a hormone produced only by females
LIGAMENT: a band of tissue that connects or supports bones and joints

★ CHAPTER 4 ★

What You Can Do to Improve

A center needs lots of energy to outplay her opponent. Shooting, blocking, and running are tough with a tired body. A guard running low on fuel won't have the power to steal balls, dribble at top speed, and feed the ball to her forwards. You play your strongest, smartest, and safest when you eat and drink the right foods at the right time.

Before the Game

Two to three hours before you hit the court, hit the kitchen or cafeteria to fuel up. Avoid simple **carbohydrates** found in candy bars and cookies. Your body will use these foods up in no time. Instead, choose complex carbohydrates. These carbs will give you energy that will keep you going into overtime. Some good choices include:

• raw broccoli, cucumbers and carrots with dip

• apple slices with cheese or peanut butter

• a sandwich on whole grain bread

• black beans with a bowl of
  grains, such as rice
  or quinoa

• a bowl of pasta

Get ready to sweat! Sweating is how your body keeps from overheating. Be sure to drink before game time. This will help make up for all the liquid you'll lose as you run up and down the court. Without enough fluid, **dehydration** robs you of energy and makes your muscles want to sit on the bench. And stick with water. As much as you might want a cold can of soda, the bubbles will fill you up before you're fully hydrated. The sugar will make you feel energized now, but you'll be sleepy by halftime.

CARBOHYDRATE: a substance that gives you energy

DEHYDRATION: a condition caused by a lack of water

Tip: The average person loses around 32 fluid ounces (.9 liters) of sweat per hour of exercise. So be sure to drink enough water!

During the Game

Sip from your water bottle whenever you get the chance to rest. If you get hungry on the court, munch on foods that will help rehydrate your body. These courtside energy boosters will help you feel full and hydrated at the same time:

- fruit, such as grapes, watermelon, pineapple, cherries, or orange slices
- brothy soup
- vegetables, such as lettuce, tomatoes, cucumbers, or celery
- 100-percent cranberry or grape juice

On extra hot or busy days, try a sports drink. These drinks contain carbohydrates and **electrolytes**. This blend gives your muscles some extra staying power. But avoid energy drinks. They are packed with caffeine and won't help your performance. In fact, they might make you jumpy and nervous.

Tip: One study found that kids ages 9 to 16 don't get enough to drink during exercise. In fact, most are already dehydrated before exercise even begins.

After the Game

After a game or practice you may not feel hungry. But your muscles are craving food. They need extra fuel to rebuild and recover from all that work. The sooner they get it, the better! Water, fresh fruit, and a **protein**-packed snack, such as a tuna sandwich, yogurt, or nuts, would do the trick. Some other good after-the-game foods include:

- a hard-boiled egg
- a peanut butter and banana sandwich made with whole-grain bread
- a salad with grilled chicken and raspberry vinaigrette
- a baked potato

ELECTROLYTE: a substance that controls or affects fluid balance in the body

PROTEIN: a substance found in foods such as meat, cheese, eggs, and fish

BASKETS OF FRUIT ★

For a healthy and fruit-filled snack, try making these baskets of fruit for your teammates. With a mixture of complex carbohydrates, protein, and fruit, they're the perfect pick-me-up before or after a game.

INGREDIENTS

nonstick cooking spray
3 tablespoons (45 milliliters) butter
½ cup (120 mL) peanut butter
40 regular marshmallows, or 4 cups (.96 L) mini marshmallows

6 cups (1.4 liters) puffed whole-grain cereal
washed fruit, such as grapes, blueberries and strawberries

SUPPLIES

muffin pan for making 24 muffins
large microwave-safe bowl

mixing spoon

Step 1: Spray the muffin pan with nonstick cooking spray.

Step 2: Combine butter, peanut butter, and marshmallows in the bowl. Microwave 1 minute or until marshmallows are melted.

Step 3: Stir to combine. Pour cereal into the bowl and stir until well blended. Cereal should be coated with the marshmallow mixture.

Step 4: Using your fingers, press cereal mixture around the bottom and sides of a muffin cup. Add more cereal until the cup is completely lined. Repeat until all the cereal is used up.

Step 5: Refrigerate muffin pan for five minutes.

Step 6: Use a butter knife or spoon to pop the now-hardened basket shapes out of the muffin cups.

Step 7: Fill each basket with fruit and serve.

Tip: The cereal mixture hardens quickly, so work fast!

Tip: If the cereal mixture sticks to your fingers, try dipping your hands in water or spraying them with nonstick spray.

CHAPTER 5 ★

Fun Off the Court

Basketball is about more than winning games. It's about making friends who will stick around even after the end-of-season trophies have been handed out. Stay in shape together by doing things as a group. Meet at a local playground or gym to keep your skills fresh. Try some one-on-one, half-court hoops, or even a game of H-O-R-S-E.

Do more than shoot hoops together. Go for a hike or a run. Exercise a different set of muscles by meeting at the local skating rink, bowling alley, or swimming pool. Or put away the sports equipment and organize team activities that give you time for more talk and less action. Have a sleepover or rainy-day craft party. The better you know one another off the court, the better you'll play together on game day.

Girls play basketball for many reasons. Some people play to be with their friends. Others want to be more fit and basketball fills their fitness needs. Still others work toward a future spot in the WNBA. Even if you just like to H-O-R-S-E around with your friends, basketball can give you the skills you need on and off the court. Whatever your level of play, basketball will strengthen your body, self-confidence, and best of all, friendships.

Craft

FLEECY JEWELRY POUCH ★

Before you head out onto the court you'll need to take off your jewelry. Do you stuff your valuables into a shoe? Or risk losing them in your locker? Instead, try keeping them in this four-pocketed jewelry pouch! Use fleece in your team colors for extra impact.

WHAT YOU'LL NEED:

two ¼-yard (23-centimeter) pieces of fleece fabric in two colors

large round dinner plate

permanent marker

scissors

small plate

straight pins

ruler

needle and thread

18-inch (46-cm) piece of ribbon or yarn

Step 1: Lay both pieces of fleece on a flat work surface.

Step 2: Set the large plate on top of one piece of fleece. Trace and cut out the large shape.

Step 3: Set the small plate on top of the other piece of fleece. Trace and cut out the small shape.

Step 4: Center the small piece of fabric over the larger piece. Secure with pins.

Step 5: Use ruler and marker to draw a line straight across the small circle. Repeat, making a line going the opposite direction of the first.

Step 6: Sew along the lines. Remove straight pins.

Step 7: Use scissors to cut 16 small, evenly-spaced holes between the large and small circles.

Step 8: Thread ribbon through the holes. Pull tight.

Sewing by Hand:

Slide the thread through the eye of the needle.

Tie the end of the thread into a knot.

Poke the needle through the underside of the fabric.

Pull the thread through the fabric to knotted end.

Poke your needle back through the fabric and up again to make a stitch.

Continue weaving the needle in and out of the fabric, making small stitches in a straight line.

When you are finished sewing, make a loose stitch.

Thread the needle through the loop and pull tight.

Cut off remaining thread.

GLOSSARY

carbohydrate (kar-boh-HYE-drate)—a substance found in foods such as bread, rice, cereal, and potatoes that gives you energy

coordination (koh-OR-duh-nay-shun)—the ability to control body movements

dehydration (dee-hy-DRAY-shuhn)—a life-threatening medical condition caused by a lack of water

electrolyte (i-LEK-truh-lite)—a substance that controls or affects fluid balance in the body

estrogen (es-TRUH-juhn)—a hormone produced only by females

field goal (FEELD GOHL)—a successful shot taken from the court while the game is in play; if shot from in front of the three-point line, these are worth two points; if shot from behind the three-point line, these are worth three points

gravity (GRAV-uh-tee)—force that pulls objects with mass together; gravity pulls objects down toward the center of Earth

ligament (LIG-uh-muhnt)—a band of tissue that connects or supports bones or joints

protein (PROH-teen)—a substance found in foods, such as meat, cheese, eggs, and fish

violation (vye-oh-LAY-shun)—an action that breaks the rules of a sport or game

READ MORE

Hunt, Sara. *Stay Fit: Your Guide to Staying Active.* Healthy Me. Mankato, Minn.: Capstone Press, 2011.

Macy, Sue. *Basketball Belles: How Two Teams and One Scrappy Player Put Women's Hoops on the Map.* New York: Holiday House, 2011.

Robinson, Tom. *Basketball. Girls Play to Win.* Chicago: Norwood House Press, 2011.

INTERNET SITES

FactHound offers a safe, fun way to find Internet sites related to this book. All of the sites on FactHound have been researched by our staff.

Here's all you do:

Visit *www.facthound.com*

Type in this code: 9781429676700

 Check out projects, games and lots more at **www.capstonekids.com**

QUIZ ANSWERS: 1. d 2. b 3. a 4. c 5. b 6. a 7. c 8. d 9. a 10. d

INDEX